Traveling in Space

Sue Becklake

Troll Associates

Library of Congress Cataloging-in-Publication Data

Becklake, Sue.
    Traveling in space / by Sue Becklake.
       p.   cm.—(Exploring the universe)
    Summary: Surveys space exploration, focusing on the flights of
rockets, satellites, and probes, and the possibility of living in
space cities.
    ISBN 0-8167-2136-X (lib. bdg.)   ISBN 0-8167-2137-8 (pbk.)
    1. Astronautics—Juvenile literature. 2. Space flight—Juvenile
literature. [1. Astronautics. 2. Space flight.] I. Title. II. Series.
TL793.B373 1991
629.4—dc20   90-11017

Published by Troll Associates

Edited by Neil Morris
Design by Sally Boothroyd
Picture research by Veneta Bullen

Printed in the U.S.A.

10 9 8 7 6 5 4 3 2 1

Illustrations:
Rhoda & Robert Burns/Drawing Attention front cover,
   pp 4, 18, 20, 21, 22-23, 24, 25
Paul Doherty pp 28-29
Chris Forsey pp 14, 15
Julia Osorno p 6
Raymond Turvey pp 7, 8-9, 10-11, 12, 13, 27

Picture credits:
Akira Fujii pp 2-3
NASA back cover, pp 1, 5, 10-11, 15, 17, 19, 26,
   31 (top)
Bernard Paris/Arianespace p 9
TASS pp 16, 30, 31 (bottom)

Front cover: an American space shuttle.
Back cover: an astronaut outside his space shuttle.
Title page: an astronaut controls his movement in space.
Pages 2-3: the constellation of Sagittarius.

Contents

Exploring space

Have you ever wondered what it would be like to travel in space? Imagine yourself strapped in your seat as your spacecraft blasts off. You feel the violent shaking of the rocket engines, and you are pushed down hard in your seat because you are gaining speed so fast. As the spacecraft rises swiftly, the air gets thinner – until there is none left and you are in space. Up there everything is weightless, so you float out of your seat when you undo the straps.

The first person to travel in space was a Russian, Yuri Gagarin, who circled the Earth in 1961, only four years after the Soviet Union launched the world's first manmade satellite, Sputnik 1. A satellite is anything in space that circles around something else. So the Moon is a satellite of Earth, and the planets, including Earth, are satellites of the Sun.

▼ Space stations and space shuttles circle close to the Earth. Satellites orbit at many different heights, often very high above the Earth. Space probes fly right away to explore other planets.

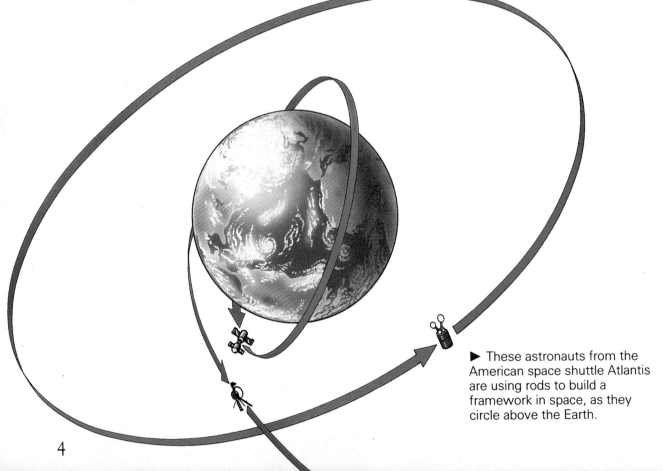

▶ These astronauts from the American space shuttle Atlantis are using rods to build a framework in space, as they circle above the Earth.

Distances in space are too enormous to imagine. Our nearest neighbor, the Moon, is about 240,000 miles away. The Sun is 93 million miles from Earth, and the next nearest star is over 250,000 times further.

Astronauts have not yet traveled beyond the Moon. The first person to set foot on the Moon was the American astronaut, Neil Armstrong, in 1969. However, we have sent robot spacecraft, called space probes, to visit distant planets such as Uranus and Neptune. Probes and satellites help scientists learn about the universe by collecting information and sending back pictures. One day they may even find other life out there.

Into space and home again

Why do spacecraft need such powerful rockets to launch them into space? An invisible force called gravity pulls everything on Earth down toward the center of the Earth. If you jump up, gravity pulls you down again. If you drop something, it always falls to the ground. Spacecraft need a speed of over 25,000 miles per hour, 20 times faster than Concorde, to escape from this pull. Satellites and space stations only need to go about 12 times as fast as Concorde, because they do not escape completely. Gravity holds them in their orbits as they circle the Earth.

▼ When you throw a ball, it always falls back down to the ground. The harder you throw the ball, the further it goes. If you could throw it with the power of a space rocket, it would escape from the Earth's gravity and fly away into space.

◄ When a spacecraft returns from space and enters the Earth's atmosphere, it gets very hot. The outside of the spacecraft and the air around it glow red hot, and it looks like a shooting star. Then it cools again as the air slows it down.

▼ The Soviet Soyuz spacecraft use huge parachutes to slow them as they fall to the ground. Then small jets fire just before landing to soften the bump.

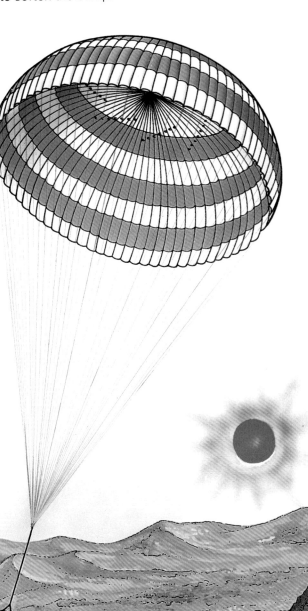

Spacecraft travel very fast in space – so fast that if they did not slow down before re-entering the Earth's atmosphere, they would burn up. As the spacecraft rubs against the air, both the air and the spacecraft glow red hot (just as rubbing your hands together makes them warm). Some spacecraft, and the astronauts inside, are protected by a heat shield. This is a thick layer that partly burns away, using up the heat. An American space shuttle has special tiles that absorb heat, instead of burning away. Only a few of them need replacing after each flight.

Rockets

The huge rockets that launch astronauts and satellites into space work just like firework rockets. Fuel burns inside the rocket, making hot gases which rush out at the back and push the rocket forward. The same thing happens if you blow up a balloon and let it go. The air rushes out and the balloon shoots off in the opposite direction.

Space rockets are powerful because they burn enormous amounts of fuel very quickly. Nine tenths of their weight is fuel and oxygen (the fuel will not burn without oxygen gas). Aircraft engines use oxygen from the air, but rockets carry their own supply. This is why rocket engines will work in space, where there is no air, but aircraft engines will not.

Most rockets have two or three stages, which are just separate rockets stacked on top of each other. Each stage drops away when its fuel is used up, and then the next stage takes over. This means that the rocket does not waste fuel by carrying unnecessary weight into space. The used stages drop into the sea or the desert. Later stages may burn up when they fall back into the Earth's atmosphere.

▼ The European Ariane rocket can carry two large satellites into space. It sometimes uses booster rockets to give its first stage extra power.

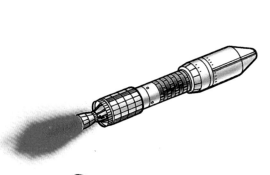

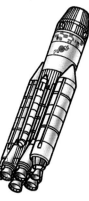

▲ When it is about 30 miles above the Earth, the first stage is pushed away. The second stage takes over and carries the satellites inside the nose cone into space. The second stage later comes off also.

▲ The third stage takes the satellites into orbit, and then it falls away with the nose cone. The satellites often go into a long thin orbit reaching from near the Earth to very high up. When the satellite is at the top of this orbit, it fires its own motors to keep it in a high orbit.

▼ An Ariane rocket is launched at Kourou in French Guiana, South America.

Space shuttles

Rockets are very expensive to build and are only used once. A space shuttle can fly into space and land on Earth again many times, making space travel more economical.

The United States has several shuttles that take off upward, like a rocket. They have a huge tank full of fuel and oxygen to feed their main rocket engines. These are helped by two large rocket boosters that burn a rubbery solid fuel, which gets used up in about two minutes. The rocket boosters then parachute down to the sea, where a waiting ship tows them back to be refueled and used again.

▼ Little jets push the used booster rockets away from the shuttle.

▼ The empty fuel tank separates in space and burns up when it re-enters the atmosphere.

An American shuttle can carry up to seven astronauts into space, as well as a cargo of satellites and other items. It circles the Earth for about a week, while the crew release the satellites and work in space.

The Russian shuttle Buran ("Snowstorm") has flown into space and back without any crew on board. It does not have any main rocket engines of its own. Instead, it is launched by a powerful rocket named Energia.

▼ When the shuttle returns to Earth, it re-enters the atmosphere underside first, glowing red hot.

▼ The shuttle lands on a runway without using its engines, like a giant glider.

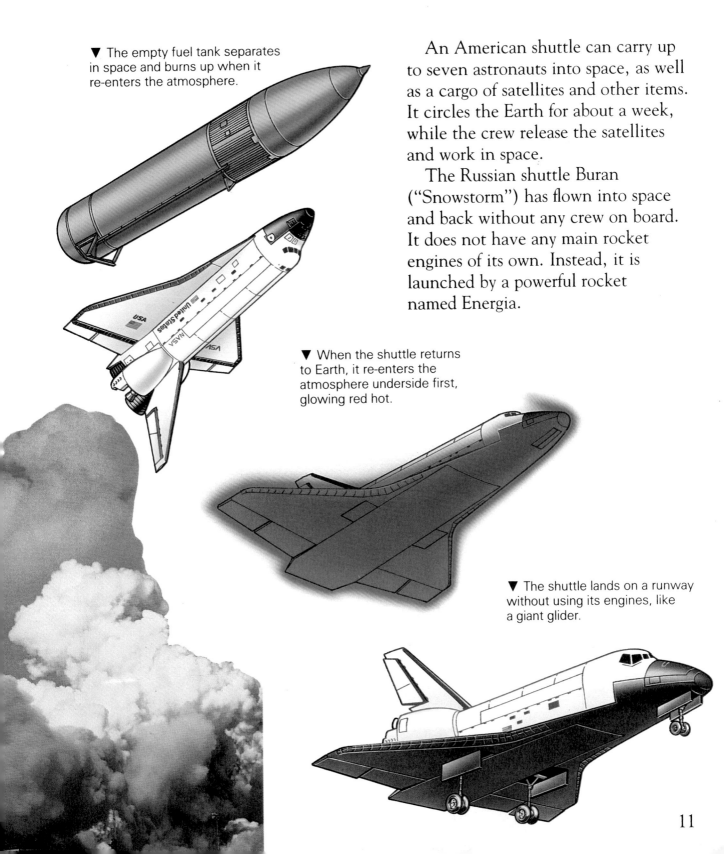

Space stations

A space station orbiting the Earth is the astronauts' home in space, so it must hold everything they need to stay alive. All their air, food, and water have to be brought up from Earth. Space stations have to have inner and outer walls to keep the air in, because there is no air outside. They also provide protection against dust and small rocks speeding through space. Inside, there are places to sleep, a toilet, a wash basin or shower, and exercise machines. There are controls for flying the space station and places to work. Sometimes there are separate laboratories.

The main part of the Russian space station, Mir, where the cosmonauts live, was launched in 1986. Then in 1987 a work module, called Kvant, was launched and joined up with Mir in space. Two more modules were added in 1989 and 1990, and there is room for more modules to be added. Cosmonauts travel up to Mir in a Soyuz spacecraft, which docks and remains fixed to the space station until they return to Earth, maybe months later. While they are there, they sometimes receive visits from other cosmonauts. Supplies and letters from their families are delivered to them by Progress supply ships.

▼ The middle part of this picture shows the main Mir space station. Here the cosmonauts (Soviet astronauts) eat, sleep, wash, exercise, and control their space station. The Kvant module, with its telescopes and instruments for studying space, is fixed to the lefthand end of Mir. On the right is a Soyuz spacecraft that brings the cosmonauts up from Earth and takes them home again.

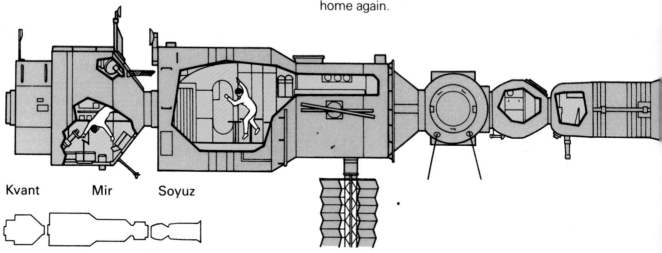

Kvant   Mir   Soyuz

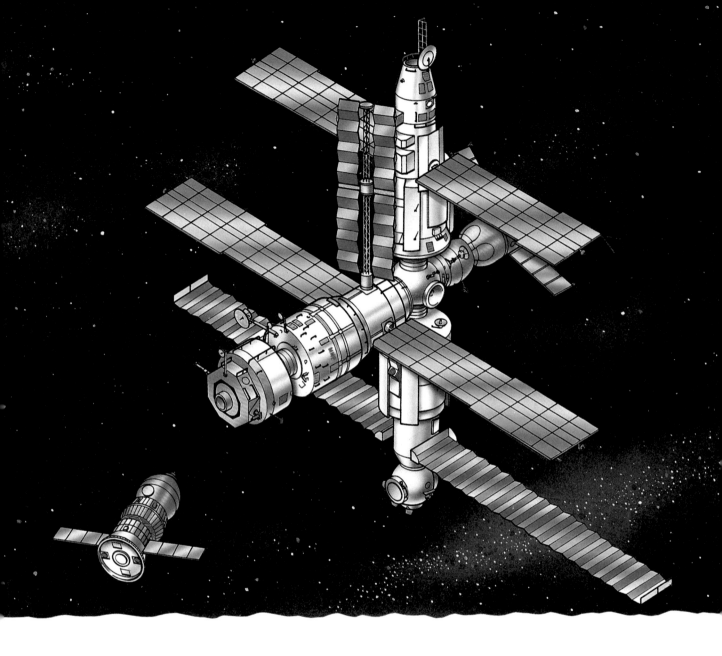

Three separate crews of astronauts lived in the American space station; Skylab during 1973 and 1974. They studied the Sun, the effects of weather and pollution on the Earth, and the ways living in space affected their own bodies.

▲ An unmanned Progress spacecraft brings supplies of food, water, air, and fuel from Earth up to Mir. It will dock with Kvant, opposite the Soyuz spacecraft at the other end of Mir. The other modules are packed with equipment for the cosmonauts to use when they work. The space station gets its electricity supply from the long solar panels sticking out from the sides.

Living in space

The trouble with living in space is that everything floats, even the astronauts. Here on Earth, gravity pulls everything down to the ground. In space, there is so little gravity that if you drop something it just floats away. This weightlessness means there is no "up" or "down," so you can sleep against a wall or even upside down. But you have to strap yourself into a sleeping bag; otherwise you would float away.

Most space food is dried to save weight. Before eating, water is added to the food packets, which can then be warmed in an oven. Some space food, such as biscuits and fresh and canned fruit, is the same as on Earth. Knives, forks, and spoons are magnetic, so they stick to the meal trays. In fact, everything must be fixed down with magnets, clips, or tapes. The astronauts have special footholds to stop them from shooting backward every time they push a button.

Weightlessness changes the astronauts' bodies slightly, and they have to exercise every day on a cycling machine or treadmill to keep fit. Their faces get puffy and, without gravity squashing their backbones, they get a little taller. But they soon return to normal once they are back on Earth.

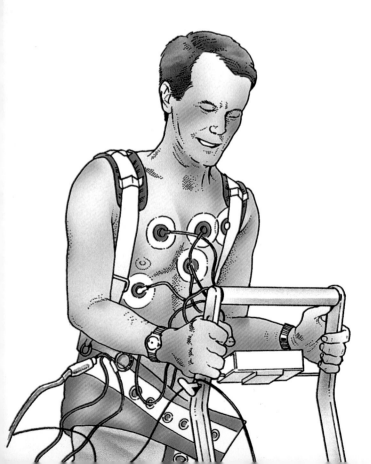

◄ A space shuttle astronaut takes exercise by running fast on a treadmill. The wires taped to his body go to instruments which measure the effects of weightlessness on his body.

▲ Space shuttle astronauts have to hold on to their bread to stop it floating away while they have a meal.

▶ Astronauts eat and drink from packets and cans fixed to food trays.

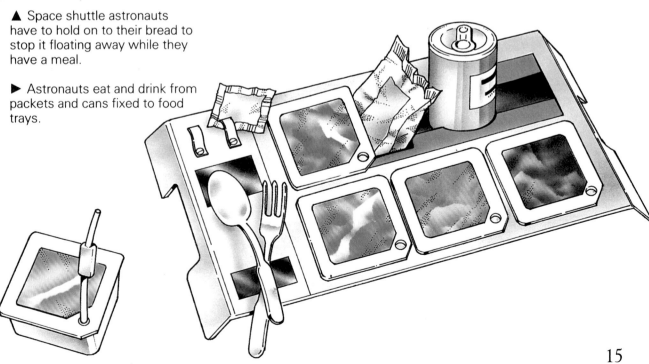

Working in space

Astronauts on board space stations and shuttles have many different jobs to keep them busy. They use cameras to photograph the Earth, and telescopes to observe distant stars and other, more mysterious objects. They study space near the Earth as they fly through it, taking measurements and collecting space dust.

Some things are very difficult to make on Earth, where gravity churns up hot liquids and keeps heavy liquids from mixing evenly with light ones. In space, where there is almost no gravity, different metals can be melted together to make light but strong materials needed for aircraft engines. The large, pure crystals used in making computers and solar cells grow better in space, and ingredients for medicines can be made in a very pure form, too. Astronauts have successfully carried out many experiments like these. In the future, there will even be factories in space.

Scientists want to know how weightlessness affects all living things. So astronauts have taken small animals, including mice, spiders, flies, moths, and bees, into space to see how they behave. They have grown plants to find out if future space travelers could grow their own food. They also check to see how weightlessness is affecting their own bodies.

◀ Svetlana Savitskaya wore a space suit to work outside the Soviet space station Salyut 7 in 1984. She was the first woman to work outside in space.

▶ William Fisher has his feet firmly fixed to the space shuttle Discovery while he holds on to the Syncom satellite. Shuttle astronauts captured the satellite from space, repaired it, and then returned it to its orbit.

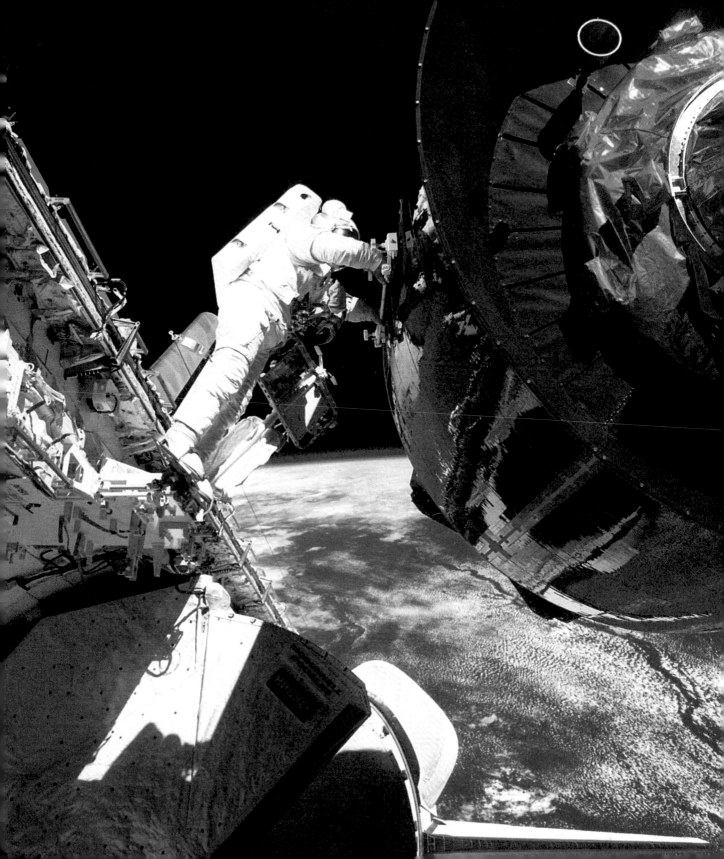

Space suits and space walks

When astronauts leave the safety of the spacecraft, they have to wear space suits to stay alive. A space suit is like a mini-spacecraft, supplying air and protection from dangerous radiation and speeding dust. It also presses down on the body – just as the atmosphere on Earth does – to stop air from bubbling out of the bloodstream, which would be fatal.

A space suit has to be very bulky to keep out the cold of space and the heat of the Sun, so there are tucks and folds in the layers of material to make it easier for the astronauts to move their arms and legs. Underneath the space suit, next to the skin, there is a cooling suit with small tubes carrying water to take away body heat. The helmet has a dark visor to protect the eyes from ultraviolet light from the Sun, and earphones and a microphone for talking with other astronauts. The backpack carries supplies of both air and water.

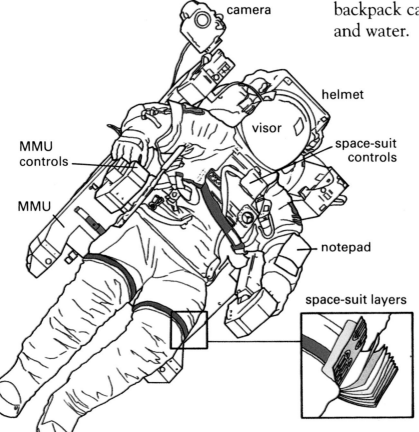

camera

helmet

visor

space-suit controls

MMU controls

MMU

notepad

space-suit layers

▶ This astronaut can move freely through space, pushed by the 24 little jets of the Manned Maneuvering Unit (MMU) fixed to his backpack. His hands control movement in any direction.

◀ The outer layer of a space suit is very tough so it won't tear. It covers several layers that insulate the astronaut from the icy cold of space. Next is a double layer with air inside, like a man-shaped balloon, pressing on his body. Underneath all this is a cooling suit with tubes full of water to carry away the astronaut's body heat.

Sealed inside their space suits, astronauts can work in space for several hours, tied to the spacecraft to stop them from floating away. To go further from their spacecraft, space-shuttle astronauts wear a Manned Maneuvering Unit (or MMU) on their back. This has little jets to move or turn them in any direction. They can even go out and capture a satellite, then bring it back to the shuttle for repairs.

Manmade satellites

Today, the Earth is surrounded by hundreds of manmade satellites. Some send telephone calls around the world; others collect information for weather forecasters and other scientists. Their orbits around the Earth are all elliptical (oval-shaped), but the orbits are not all at the same height or at the same angle to the equator.

Satellites need electricity to run their instruments. This usually comes from solar cells, like the ones on solar-powered calculators, which turn sunlight into electricity. Hundreds of solar cells are needed to make enough electricity to run a satellite. They either cover the satellite's body or are attached to huge, winglike solar panels.

▲ This huge satellite, taller than a house, sends TV signals and up to 270,000 telephone calls at once between Europe and the USA. Its curved sides are covered with solar cells to provide the satellite with electricity. The saucer-shaped antennas send and receive radio signals from Earth.

◄ Large antennas on the ground point up at the satellite, 22,300 miles above the Earth, catching its signals and passing them on to TV transmitters and telephone exchanges.

Controllers on Earth use radio signals to send instructions to a satellite and to collect information from it. The signals travel to and from antennas on the satellite and on the ground. These antennas are often shaped like saucers.

Satellites must keep their antennas facing the Earth and their instruments pointing at the right target. They have sensors that act like eyes and "look" for the Earth, the Sun, or bright stars. The sensors tell the satellite when it is pointing in the wrong direction. Then small jets shoot out gas to turn the satellite to the right direction again.

Satellites at work

Satellites now bring us live television programs from all over the world, beaming them directly to our homes. They also send telephone calls and business information across the oceans. These all travel as radio signals from large antennas on the ground up to the satellite and down to the receiving antennas. The satellites circle in a special orbit, 22,300 miles above the equator, where they keep pace with the Earth's spin. They therefore seem to keep still in the sky, and antennas on Earth can stay pointing at a satellite all the time.

▲ Satellites have many different shapes. *From left to right*: Meteosat spins around as it watches the weather; Spot takes pictures of the Earth; the Hubble Space Telescope looks much further out into space than the largest telescopes on Earth; and Olympus sends TV and telephone signals around the world.

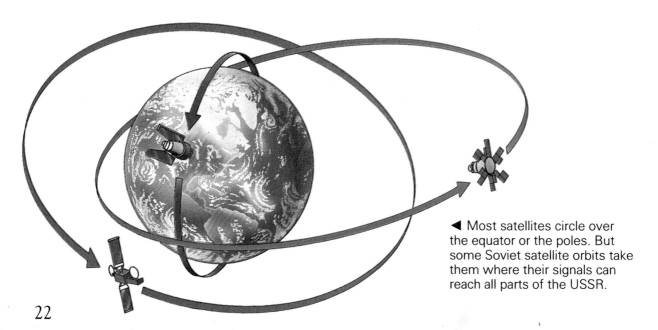

◄ Most satellites circle over the equator or the poles. But some Soviet satellite orbits take them where their signals can reach all parts of the USSR.

Weather satellites look down at the clouds and take measurements that help to forecast the weather. Other satellites help to map remote areas, check that crops are healthy, or spot pollution, forest fires, and areas that might be drilled for oil. Their orbits usually pass over the poles, and they "see" almost the whole Earth as it spins below.

Astronomers use satellites to study objects far away in space, collecting X rays and other rays that cannot get through the atmosphere to the ground. Navigation satellites tell travelers (in boats and planes, for example) where they are, and can even give the height and speed of aircraft. Some countries use spy satellites to take photographs of other countries or to listen to other people's radio messages.

Space explorers

Space probes have explored the planets, many of their moons, and Halley's Comet. They fly past their target, orbit around it, or sometimes even land on it. They have visited all the planets except the furthest, Pluto.

Voyager 2 has flown past the four giant planets, Jupiter, Saturn, Uranus, and Neptune. It took close-up pictures of them and some of their moons, discovering many new ones and sending back huge quantities of information that astronomers couldn't have gathered from Earth.

The two nearest planets, Venus and Mars, have been explored by probes that landed on the surface. The Venera probes to Venus had to be very tough, because Venus is incredibly hot. Also, the atmosphere presses down 90 times harder than on Earth, and there is acid in its thick clouds. On Mars, the Viking Landers scooped up soil and tested it for signs of life. But the results did not prove whether there is any life on Mars.

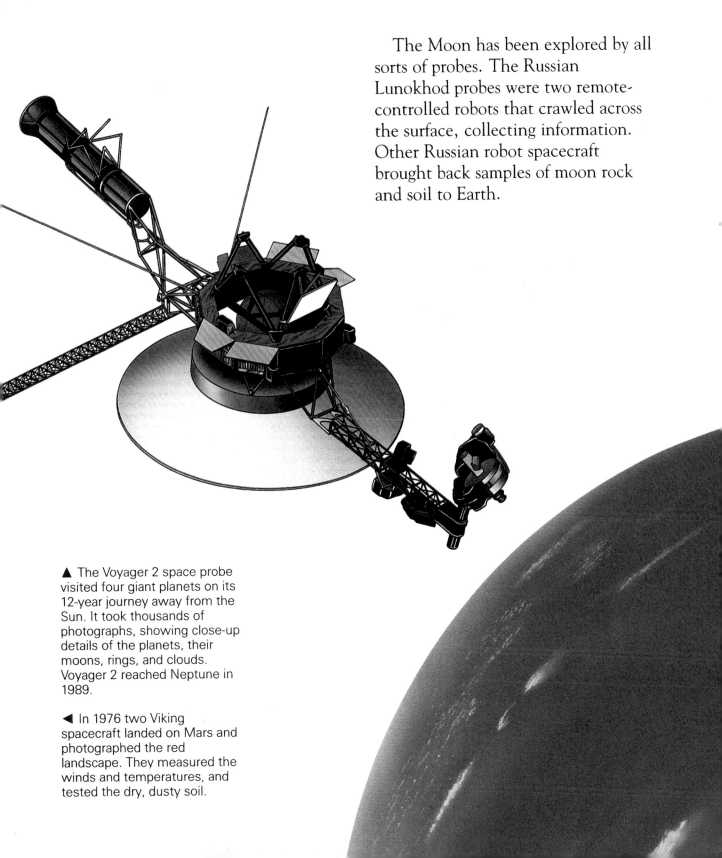

The Moon has been explored by all sorts of probes. The Russian Lunokhod probes were two remote-controlled robots that crawled across the surface, collecting information. Other Russian robot spacecraft brought back samples of moon rock and soil to Earth.

▲ The Voyager 2 space probe visited four giant planets on its 12-year journey away from the Sun. It took thousands of photographs, showing close-up details of the planets, their moons, rings, and clouds. Voyager 2 reached Neptune in 1989.

◄ In 1976 two Viking spacecraft landed on Mars and photographed the red landscape. They measured the winds and temperatures, and tested the dry, dusty soil.

Man on the Moon

The only place people have actually visited in space is the Moon. Between 1969 and 1972 American astronauts visited six different parts of the Moon, but no one has been there since.

Each time, three astronauts traveled to the Moon in an Apollo command module launched from Earth by a huge Saturn 5 rocket. One of the astronauts circled the Moon in the command module, while the others landed on the surface in a lunar module.

In their bulky space suits, they found hopping around easier than walking. They collected soil and rocks, picking them up with tongs or scoops because they couldn't bend down. Once they had completed their experiments, the lunar module took them back to the command module. Then the astronauts set off on their three-day journey back to Earth, leaving the lunar module behind.

Altogether, astronauts have brought back nearly 850 pounds of moon rock for scientists to study. On their last three visits they took a moon car, the Lunar Roving Vehicle, with them so they could explore further. They also left instruments on the Moon – one to listen for moonquakes ("earthquakes" on the Moon), and another to measure the distance to the Moon by reflecting laser light back to Earth. These experiments continued working long after the astronauts returned home, sending results back to Earth by radio.

◄ On the last trip to the Moon, the Apollo 17 astronauts explored a mountain valley. They traveled nearly 21 miles in their Lunar Rover, collecting about 240 pounds of moon rock.

► A giant Saturn 5 rocket blasts off with the power of 160 jumbo jet engines, sending Apollo astronauts on their three-day journey to the Moon.

Mars and the future

The next place astronauts are likely to visit is Mars. It is further than Venus (it will take at least six months to get there), but much safer to land on. Mars can supply very little, so their spacecraft will have to carry supplies for the whole journey. Outside the spacecraft the astronauts will need to wear space suits because there is not enough oxygen in the air to breathe.

Space flight is extremely expensive, and engineers are looking for more economical ways of getting into space. Future space planes will be used many times, like shuttles. But they will take off on a runway like a plane, not upward like a rocket. Some plans show the space plane riding almost all the way into space on the back of a launching plane. Another type, Hotol, is a single space plane with engines that work in air as well as in space.

In the future, people may possibly live on the Moon or Mars, or in huge space cities orbiting the Earth. On the Moon or Mars, they would live inside protective buildings filled with air and wear space suits outside. Future jobs on the Moon could include astronomy and mining materials needed on Earth or for space factories.

Life in a space city would be very much like life on Earth, with landscapes of trees and plants, and normal day and night. The city would spin slowly to make you feel heavy, just as gravity does on Earth.

People may live in space cities sooner than we imagine. Already, Russian cosmonauts have lived in space for over a year. And only a few years before the first trip to the Moon, space travel still seemed an impossible dream.

▶ Today space stations orbit the Earth, and one day you or your children may live in space. Space shuttles could carry you up to the space station. People could live and work on the Moon or Mars in buildings like these.

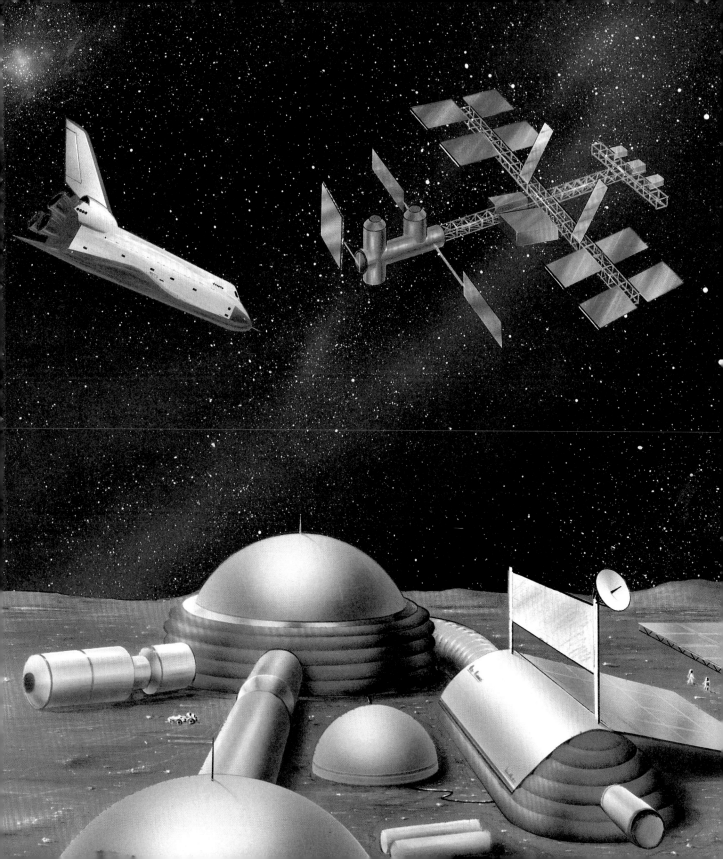

Fact file

Space history

1957 The first manmade satellite, Sputnik 1, was launched by the Soviet Union. Sputnik 2 carried the first animal, a dog named Laika, into space.
1958 The first American satellite, Explorer 1, was launched.
1959 The Soviet Luna 3 space probe flew behind the Moon and sent back pictures of the far side, which cannot be seen from Earth.
1961 On April 12th, Soviet cosmonaut Yuri Gagarin became the first man in space. He circled the Earth once in Vostok 1. On May 5th, Alan Shepard was the first American in space: his flight in Mercury 3 lasted 15 minutes.
1962 Mariner 2 flew past Venus. It was the first successful probe to another planet.
1963 Valentina Tereshkova became the first woman in space.
1965 Alexei Leonov was the first person to leave a spacecraft in flight. His space walk from Voskhod 2 lasted ten minutes.
1968 Apollo 8 was the first manned spacecraft to orbit the Moon.
1969 Apollo 11 made the first manned Moon landing. Neil Armstrong was the first man to set foot on the Moon.
1970 Unmanned Luna 16 brought moon rock back to Earth. The robot moon rover, Lunokhod 1, crawled over the Moon's surface.
1971 The first space station, Salyut 1, was launched into Earth orbit.
1972 Last Apollo mission to the Moon. Astronauts spent 76 hours on the lunar surface.
1973 Skylab, the largest space station, was launched into Earth orbit.

1975 An American Apollo spacecraft joined up with a Russian Soyuz spacecraft, 140 miles above the Earth – the first international cooperation in space.
1981 First flight of the American space shuttle Columbia.
1983 Space probe Pioneer 10 became the first manmade object to leave the solar system, carrying a message from people on Earth.
1984 Space shuttle astronauts performed the first satellite repair, capturing the satellite Solar Max and later returning it to orbit.
1986 American space shuttle Challenger exploded soon after launch, killing all seven crew members.
1987-88 Russian cosmonauts Vladimir Titov and Musa Manarov spent almost exactly a year in space on the Mir space station.
1989 Voyager 2 probe reached Neptune after a 12-year journey.

▼ The first man in space, Yuri Gagarin, in his spacecraft in 1961.

▶ Neil Armstrong photographed Edwin Aldrin as he became the second man to step onto the Moon in 1969.

Apollo Moon program
In 1961 President Kennedy announced the Apollo program, to design and build a rocket and spacecraft that could land men on the Moon by 1970. There were four manned Apollo test flights, two in Earth orbit and two to Moon orbit and back, before Apollo 11 landed the first men on the Moon in 1969. Six more flights followed, five successful Moon landings and the near disaster of Apollo 13 when the astronauts only just managed to return to Earth after an explosion on their spacecraft.

back information for a short time. Orbiting probes have mapped the surface through the clouds, using radar. Two Viking probes landed on **Mars** in 1976, testing the soil for signs of life and watching the weather. Voyagers 1 and 2 flew past **Jupiter** in 1979, and **Saturn** in 1980 and 1981. Voyager 2 went on to reach **Uranus** in 1986 and **Neptune** in 1989. The probes discovered more moons around each planet, and sent back close-up pictures of the planets, many of their moons, and enough information to keep scientists busy for many years.

▼ The powerful Soviet rocket Energia on the launch pad.

Space rubbish

When one of the hundreds of satellites circling the Earth stops working, it may gradually circle closer to Earth until it burns or breaks up as it hits the atmosphere. Others will stay in orbit for hundreds or thousands of years. They become space rubbish, along with other junk such as bits of rockets used for launching satellites. All this rubbish circling the Earth makes space travel more dangerous. Space rubbish left on the Moon includes six Lunar Landers, three Lunar Rovers, two Lunokhods, and many other probes from the early days of space travel.

Animals in space

The first living thing to travel in space was a dog called Laika. It did not return to Earth, but proved that animals could survive in space. Laika was followed by several dogs, monkeys, and other animals.

Exploring the planets

The only probe to visit **Mercury** was Mariner 10, which flew past it in 1973. A series of Russian Venera probes have landed on the surface of **Venus**, sending

Index